Spotlight on Reading

Cause & Effect

Grades 1–2

Frank Schaffer

An imprint of Carson-Dellosa Publishing LLC
Greensboro, North Carolina

Credits

Layout and Cover Design: Van Harris
Development House: The Research Masters

Cover Photo: Image Copyright Sonya Etchison Used under license from Shutterstock, Inc.

This book has been correlated to state, common core state, national, and Canadian provincial standards. Visit *www.carsondellosa.com* to search for and view its correlations to your standards

Frank Schaffer
An imprint of Carson-Dellosa Publishing LLC
PO Box 35665
Greensboro, NC 27425 USA
www.carsondellosa.com

ISBN 978-16-099-6483-2
04-231137784

About the Book

Mastering the skill of cause and effect will help young readers better understand stories and informational writing. Identification of these two elements in prose allows students to explain why things happen and what makes them happen.

The activities included in this workbook provide teachers with tools for instruction on and practice with cause and effect. Young readers will benefit from lessons that help them recognize stated cause and effect relationships within a sentence, across two sentences, and within a short paragraph. The activities herein will also help students recognize cause and effect in art and poetry. Students progress for low-difficulty to high-difficulty tasks while applying knowledge of cause and effect statements. Not only are these skills valuable for reading comprehension, but they also help students understand that actions have consequences.

• •

Table of Contents

Cold Hands

A **cause** is what makes something happen. An **effect** is what happens. Read each pair of sentences. Write C in front of the sentence that tells about the cause. Write E in front of the sentence that tells about the effect.

• •

1. _____ Tom was cold.

    _____ He rubbed his hands together.

2. _____ He rubbed even harder.

    _____ Rubbing made his hands warm. But he wanted them warmer!

3. _____ He rubbed faster.

    _____ That made his hands hot!

4

Pets

To find the effect, ask yourself, "What happened?" To find the cause, ask yourself, "Why?" Write the cause and the effect for each sentence.

• •

1. Miguel's dog jumped up and wagged its tail when Miguel poured food into a dish.

    What happened? Cause: _____

    Why? Effect: _____

2. Mary was happy when her cat climbed down from the tree.

    What happened? Cause: _____

    Why? Effect: _____

3. Quan's hamster climbed a toy ladder to get some cheese.

    What happened? Cause: _____

    Why? Effect: _____

4. Amy walked to the barn. She had an apple in her hand. Her pony ran to the fence.

    What happened? Cause: _____

    Why? Effect: _____

What Makes You Happy

How you feel can be an effect. The pictures on the left are causes. Circle the face on the right that tells the effect.

Cause **Effect**

1.

2.

3.

4. 

5.

Cause and Effect • CD-104550

Good Dog, Bad Dog

Look at the pictures. What does the dog do that causes Kelly to say, "Good dog"? Write **Good Dog** in the boxes under those pictures. What causes Kelly to say, "Bad dog"? Write **Bad Dog** in the boxes under those pictures.

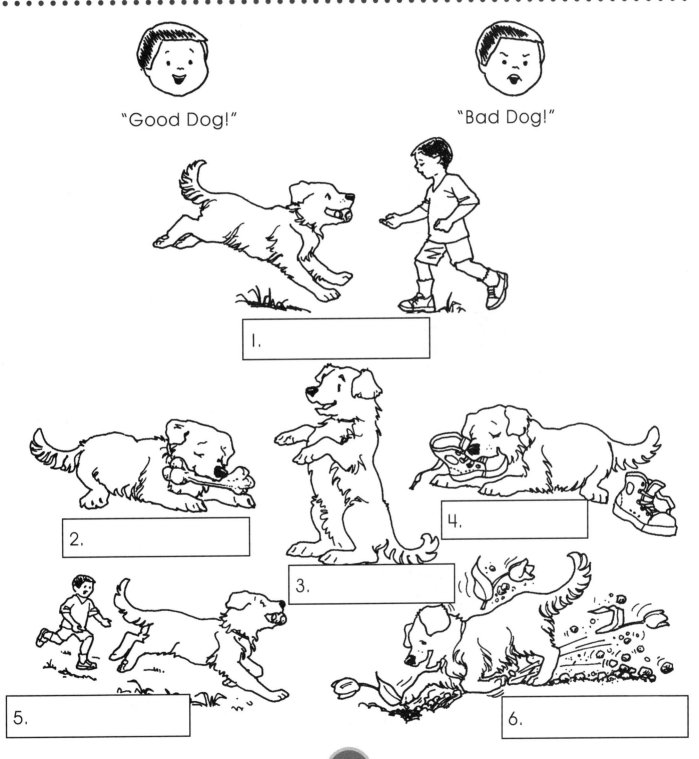

"Good Dog!"

"Bad Dog!"

1.

2.

3.

4.

5.

6.

Name _____

Read each pair of words. One word describes a cause. The other word describes an effect. Write the cause and effect on the right blanks. Use the words to complete each sentence.

• •

Example: bake, cake

Cause: ___bake_____   Effect: ___cake_____

How do you know? You bake the batter to get a cake!

1. rain, wet

Cause:_____   Effect: _____

How do you know? _____ makes you _____.

2. hot, sun

Cause:_____   Effect: _____

How do you know? _____makes you _____.

3. tree, seed

Cause: _____   Effect: _____

How do you know? You must plant a _____ to grow a _____.

Name _____

Grocery Shopping

Read the stories. Answer the cause and effect questions. Write the answers on the lines below.

• •

Meg wants pancakes. Mom has all she needs, except the syrup. She goes to the store and looks for syrup. The store is out of syrup! Mom goes to another store, then another. She cannot find syrup anywhere.

It starts to snow, so Mom has to go home. Mom is sad.

Dad is at home with Meg. He went shopping. "I bought the last of the syrup," he says.

Mom smiles. Meg smiles too. They can have pancakes now!

1. Mom had to go to a lot of stores because she _____

    _____ .

2. Mom and Meg smiled because now they _____

    _____ .

Lola is a vegetarian. She eats fruits and vegetables. She does not eat meat. She went to the store. She wanted to make a sandwich. She got tomatoes and lettuce. She got bread. She got spicy mustard. Lola went right past the meat counter. She got all of the foods she wanted. Lola made a tasty sandwich!

3. Lola went past the meat counter because she _____

    _____ .

4. Because Lola got all of the foods she wanted, she _____

    _____ .

Name _____

What to Wear?

You might wear a raincoat because it is a stormy day. The weather is the cause. What you wear is the effect. Look at each cause. Circle each effect.

	Cause	**Effect**
1.		
2.		
3.		
4.		

Cause and Effect • CD-104550

Name _____

Read each pair of sentences. Write **C** on the line by the sentence that tells about the cause. Write **E** on the line by the sentence that tells about the effect.

• •

1. The wind blows hard. _____

   Dust is in the air. _____

2. The balloon pops. _____

   Rosa blows more and more air into the balloon. _____

3. The clown keeps falling down. _____

   Everyone laughs. _____

4. We find the perfect book. _____

   We go to the library. _____

5. I turn on the lamp. _____

   It is light in the room. _____

How Would You Feel?

Look at the causes on the left. Draw a line matching each cause to the correct effect.

Cause **Effect**

1.  a.

2.  b.

3.  c.

4.  d.

Rain, Rain, Go Away!

Read the story. Answer the cause and effect questions on the next page.

• •

Shawn walked up the steps to his family's apartment. It was going to be another long, boring afternoon.

It was still raining. It had been raining for three days! There were puddles in the street and on the sidewalk.

Shawn's mom had picked him up at school. She was parking the car.

Shawn wiped his shoes on the mat outside their apartment. He saw a spider on the wall by the door. It was big and furry. It walked up the wall, but it stopped when it saw him.

Shawn stared at the spider. The spider stared at Shawn.

Shawn's mom came up the stairs. She took a big step back.

"What's wrong?" Shawn asked.

His mom pointed to the spider.

"Oh!" Shawn said. "It's just a harmless trapdoor spider. We studied them in class. All the rain must have flooded its home."

Shawn's mom looked more closely at the spider. "You are right."

"Do we have any paper?" Shawn asked.

"Why do you want paper?" his mom asked.

"I want to draw a picture of it for school."

"There is paper inside the desk in the living room," his mom said.

Shawn ran inside and grabbed paper and pencils. Today would not be a boring day after all! He loved looking at insects.

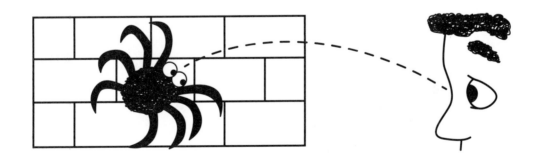

13

Rain, Rain, Go Away (cont.)

Write **C** on the line by the sentence that tells about the cause. Write **E** on the line by the sentence that tells about the effect.

• •

1. There were lots of puddles. _____

    It rained for three days. _____

2. Shawn's mom drove him home from school. _____

    She had to put the car away. _____

3. Shawn had to wipe his feet. _____

    There was mud on Shawn's shoes. _____

4. The spider climbed up the wall. _____

    The rain filled up the spider's home. _____

Weather Report

A weather report causes you to decide what to wear for the day. What you wear is the effect. Read each weather report. Circle the correct effect.

● ●

Cause

Effect

1. Today will be sunny and warm. What will you wear?

2. Today will be cooler. It will rain in the morning. What will you wear?

3. Today will be cold. It might snow. What will you wear?

Try This: On another sheet of paper draw a picture of today's weather. Draw two things the weather caused you to wear today.

Name _____

Read the story. Read each pair of sentences about the story. Circle the word **cause** by the sentence that tells about a cause. Circle the word **effect** by the sentence that tells about the effect.

• •

Have you ever thrown a rock in a pond? Did you see waves circle out from the place where the rock hit the water?

When there is an earthquake in the ocean, big waves go out from the place where it happened. There are several waves, not just one. These big waves can raise the level of the ocean.

If the waves are big enough and they hit land, they can cause problems. They can knock down buildings in towns by the shore. Do not worry. This does not always happen.

Fishermen on two boats saw a very big wave near Alaska. They rode over the wave in their boats. They were safe! That wave was the biggest ever seen by humans!

1.	Waves go out from the place where the rock fell in the water.	cause	effect
	You throw a rock into a pond.	cause	effect
2.	There is an earthquake under the ocean.	cause	effect
	Waves go out from the place where it happened.	cause	effect
3.	Fishermen floated over the wave.	cause	effect
	The fishermen were in their boats when a big wave came.	cause	effect

Name _____

Read the story. Answer the cause and effect questions by circling the correct causes.

• •

The jungle animals gave a party. It was the monkey's special day. Everyone sang and danced. The monkey got on the tree branches. He did tricks. All the animals cheered. His tricks were great! The tiger wanted everyone to cheer for him. The tiger tried to do tricks. The animals did not cheer. The tiger could stand on the tree branch. He did not know tricks!

1. The animals had a party because

    a. it was fun.   b. it was the monkey's special day.

2. The animals clapped and cheered for the monkey because

    a. his tricks were great.   b. it was his special day.

3. The animals did not clap for the tiger because

    a. he looked so silly.   b. he could not do the monkey's tricks.

What Happened?

Draw a line to match each effect to the correct cause.

Effect

1. Kate was all wet because

2. Joe's dad was mad because

3. My dog Scruff ran because

4. Keisha asked for a glass of water because

5. Toby smiled because

Cause

a. I threw his ball.

b. she was thirsty.

c. he forgot to put his bike away.

d. his mom gave him ice cream.

e. it began to rain.

Sound Effects

Sound can be a cause. Read the effects. Draw a line to match each effect with the correct cause.

• •

Effect	**Cause**

1. Dusty ran to Jason

2. Jose lined up with the kids in his class

3. The soccer teams stopped playing

4. The cowboys picked up their plates and cups

a. when the school bell rang.

b. when the cook rang the dinner bell.

c. when Jason whistled for him.

d. when the coach blew the whistle.

19

In the News

Headlines tell the effect. News stories tell the cause. Write the best headline for each story. Use the Headline Bank for ideas.

• •

Headline Bank

Wind Blows House Down

Boy Saves Dog

Huge Baby Weighed

Grass Turns Yellow

Kids Clean Up

1. A baby elephant was born on Monday. Scientists thought it must be the biggest baby born in Africa in ten years!

   Headline: _____

2. The second grade students made a mess at the school picnic. So, their teacher taught them about recycling. They did not want to leave their trash at the park.

   Headline: _____

3. There had been no rain for weeks. No one had been able to water their lawns.

   Headline: _____

4. Jeff saw a lost puppy in the park. He took it home and gave it food and water.

   Headline: _____

5. Deb made a tent in her backyard. She used old newspaper for the walls. It was fun to play in the tent. But the tent was not very strong.

   Headline: _____

Elephants in the Wild

Read the story. Answer the cause and effect questions.

• •

It was a hot day. The elephants came down to the watering hole. They wanted to get a drink. The older elephants checked for crocodiles. There were none, so it was safe. The baby elephants played in the water. It was safe, so the elephants relaxed. They began to drink the water.

A hippo came. The baby elephants ran. The older elephants made loud noises with their trunks. It sounded like trumpets. That noise made the hippo run! The baby elephants came back. The watering hole was safe again. They all enjoyed the cool water.

I. What caused the elephants to go to the watering hole?_____

_____

2. Why did the older elephants check for crocodiles?_____

_____

3. Why did the older elephants make noise? _____

_____

Ocean Waves

Read the story. Read each pair of sentences about the story. Circle the sentence that tells about the effect.

• •

Most waves are not very big. You can play in little waves at the beach. It can be fun!

Not all big waves come from earthquakes. Some waves start when there are storms at sea. The wind blows very hard for a long time. The waves get bigger and bigger. They can be eighty feet high!

Big waves can knock over the piers. Usually they do not come very far inland.

Sometimes, really big storms happen. These storms are called hurricanes. They make very big waves. These waves do come inland. The water can flood the streets! When this happens, people have to leave the beach. The beach is not safe! They can come back to the beach when the hurricane is over.

1. Wind blows across the water.

    Waves form.

2. The waves get bigger.

    The wind blows very hard for a long time.

3. People have to leave the beach.

    Hurricanes bring big waves into the streets.

Find the Clues

Clue words can help you find the cause and effect. Some clue words are **because, so, when**, and **why**. Circle the clue words in the sentences below. Use the clue to help you write the cause and effect.

• •

Example: The clock broke (when) my dog knocked it off the table.
   Cause: **my dog knocked it off the table**
   Effect: **the clock broke**

1. I did not mow the lawn, so I cannot play.

   Cause: _____

   Effect: _____

2. I fell off my bike because my tire hit a rock.

   Cause: _____

   Effect: _____

3. Mom was mad when I laughed at my brother.

   Cause: _____

   Effect: _____

4. I ran away because the dog growled at me.

   Cause: _____

   Effect: _____

5. I am your friend because you are funny and nice.

   Cause: _____

   Effect: _____

Big Mistakes

Read the stories. Answer the cause and effect questions.

• •

Will had never climbed a mountain this tall. He thought it would take all morning. It took longer than that. It took all day. What a mistake! He should have packed a lunch. He finally got to the top! He was too hungry to enjoy the view.

I. Will could not enjoy the view from the top of the mountain because ____

_____

_____

_____

Neyla thought she knew enough about the topic to make her speech. She did not make notes. The time for the speech got closer. She still did not make notes. Neyla stood at the front of the class. She could not think of a thing to say! She would never make that mistake again.

2. Neyla could not give her speech because _____

_____

_____

_____

Cause and Effect • CD-104550

Glaciers

Read the article. Match each cause with the correct effect. Write the letter of the effect on the line by the cause.

• •

Glaciers start high in the mountains where lots of snow falls. It stays cold high in the mountains. The snow does not melt. As more snow falls, the flakes pack together. This is like the way snow gets packed together to make a snowball. Snow gets packed so closely that ice forms. When more snow falls, the ice gets thicker and heavier. Then it begins to slide. The moving ice is called a glacier.

Causes

1. When the ice gets thicker and heavier, _____

2. High in the mountains where it stays cold, _____

3. When the snow packs closely, _____

4. When more snow falls, _____

Effects
a. snow falls.
b. ice forms.
c. the snow packs together.
d. it begins to slide.

My Emotions

Emotion is another word for feelings. Emotions can be effects. Read the sentences below. Draw a line to match each cause to the correct effect.

• •

Cause

Effect

1. When my friend hugged me

    a. I felt sad

2. When my friend broke my favorite toy

    b. I felt surprised

3. When the lights went out

    c. I felt loved

4. When I fell down

    d. I felt afraid

5. When all my friends threw me a party

    e. I felt angry

Name _____

Read the story. Answer the cause and effect questions.

• •

Karen and Jim were going camping with Dad. They loaded sleeping bags and a camp stove into the van. Mom filled a box with bread, peanut butter, cookies, apples, and chips. Dad carried out the ice chest and a jug of water.

"We are ready to go," he said.

When they got to the state park, Karen and Jim helped Dad set up camp.

"Bring me the tent," Dad said.

Jim looked in the van. "It's not here."

"Oh, no!" cried Karen. "We forgot the tent. We will have to go home."

"No," Dad said. "It's a nice, warm night. And it's not going to rain. We will roll our sleeping bags out on the ground. The sky will be our tent."

"Hurray!" shouted Karen and Jim.

1. Why did Karen think they would have to go home? _____

    _____

    _____

2. Why did they get to stay? _____

    _____

    _____

3. What did they use as a tent? _____

    _____

    _____

4. What do you think will happen if it rains? _____

    _____

    _____

Letter to Grandma

Read the letter. Circle the correct causes and effects to finish the sentences below.

• •

Dear Grandma,

I did not go to school today because it snowed a lot. I wanted to go outside as soon as I woke up. Mom said it was too cold.

Later, I put on my jacket, my mittens, my hat, and a scarf.

I could not go sledding because I broke my sled. I made a snowman instead. Do you like to make snowmen? I drew a picture of the snowman because it will melt soon. His eyes are pine cones. Can you guess what I used for a mouth?

Love,
Danny

1. It snowed, so Danny

   a. did not have to go to school.

   b. had to stay inside all day.

   c. could not go sledding.

   d. had to wear warm clothes.

   e. decided to make a snowman.

2. Danny put on a jacket, mittens, hat, and scarf

   a. because it was cold outside.

   b. because he was going sledding.

   c. because he was going to play in the snow.

   d. because he wanted to see Grandma.

A Picnic

Read the story. Circle the correct causes and effects to finish the sentences below.

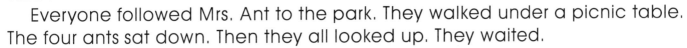

One sunny day, Mrs. Ant said, "Let's go to the park for a picnic."

"Good idea," said Mr. Ant. "Families will be eating there."

"Can we go now?" asked Art Ant. "I am hungry."

"I don't want to go," said Amy Ant.

"Why not?" asked Mrs. Ant.

"Last time we did not find any food," Amy said.

"This time we might find lots of food," said Art.

Everyone followed Mrs. Ant to the park. They walked under a picnic table. The four ants sat down. Then they all looked up. They waited.

1. The Ants went to the park for a picnic because

    a. the park was pretty.

    b. families eat in the park.

2. Art Ant wanted to go because

    a. he could play in the grass.

    b. he was hungry.

3. Amy Ant did not want to go because

    a. sometimes people do not leave food.

    b. sometimes people step on ants.

4. The Ant family sat under the picnic table and looked up

    a. to watch the sky.

    b. to wait for food to drop down.

Lisa's Big Win

Read the story. Write the answers to the cause and effect questions.

• •

Lisa and Jayla were playing in a soccer game. Lisa was good. She could make goals. Her friend Jayla was not playing well. The game was almost over. Their team was losing. Jayla was not helping out.

"You think too much," Lisa told Jayla. "Just play the ball."

Jayla frowned. Lisa felt bad. She wanted Jayla to be good too. She knew Jayla could play better. Her friend was just nervous.

Lisa got the ball. "Follow me," she told Jayla. Jayla did.

Lisa charged at the goal. The goalie jumped in front of Lisa. Lisa was a star. The goalie knew she would try to score. "Take my pass!" Lisa shouted. She kicked the ball sideways. Jayla caught it with her foot. She shot at the goal.

The ball went in!

Jayla never got another goal, but she played well. She laughed and smiled. Her team lost, but Lisa still felt like a winner because she helped a friend.

1. Why did Lisa think Jayla was not playing well?
    Lisa thought Jayla was not playing well because _____

    _____

2. What caused Lisa to pass the ball to Jayla?
    Lisa passed the ball to Jayla because _____

    _____

3. What effect did Lisa's pass have on the goalie?
    Because Lisa was a star, the goalie _____

    _____

4. What caused Lisa to feel like a winner even though they lost?
    Lisa felt like a winner because _____

    _____

Essie's Report Card

Read the story. Look at Essie's report card. Circle the answers to the cause and effect questions.

• •

Essie had ideas about how to do things. When the teacher said what to do, Essie had a better way. Once the teacher said, "glue the dried beans inside the lines." Essie knew they would be better outside the lines. The lunch monitor said, "Eat slowly." Essie ate quickly. When recess came, her friends wanted to play on the slide. Essie played on the swings instead.

Report Card			
Reading	☆	Gets along with others	☆
Writing	☆	Follows directions	☹
Spelling	☆	Listens carefully	☹
Math	☆	Mrs. Michaels	

1. What was the cause of Essie's low grades?

   a. She did things her own way.

   b. She talked too much in class.

   c. She did not get along with others.

2. Essie did not follow directions because

   a. she could not listen.

   b. she did not understand.

   c. she thought she had a better way to do things.

3. We know Essie is a good student because

   a. Mrs. Michaels gave her mostly good grades.

   b. she got a sad face in "Follows directions."

School Program

Read the story. Look at the schedule. Circle the answers to the cause and effect questions.

• •

It is the day before the school program. The teachers are ready. They took all the poetry books out of the school library. They put the books in the classrooms. The students will read poems about trees!

The teachers dug holes so that students could plant trees. The first graders made paper leaves for the costumes. They wanted to look like trees in the parade!

It is the day of the program! Here is what happens:

9:00 Students read tree poems.

9:05 Fifth graders planted four trees.

9:30 Fourth graders presented "Why We Love Trees."

9:45 First graders presented "Parade of Leaves."

10:00 Recess spent playing under the trees!

1. All the poetry books in the school library were checked out because
   a. the students love poetry.
   b. students were reading tree poems.

2. The teachers dug four deep holes the day before the program so
   a. students could plant four trees.
   b. students could jump in and out of them.

3. The first graders taped leaves on their shirts for their parade of trees so
   a. they could look funny.
   b. they could look like trees.

Windy Farm

Read the story. Circle the answers to the cause and effect questions on the next page.

• •

Three friends lived on Windy Farm. There was Harry the Horse, Duncan the Dog, and Olive the Owl. Each of them wanted to build a new house. A house would keep them safe when the wind blew.

Harry made his house out of straw. He loved to eat straw! A house made of his favorite food would be good. When the wind blew hard, his house fell over! Harry felt sad.

Duncan made his house out of sticks. He loved to fetch sticks! A house made of his favorite toy would be good. When the wind blew even harder, some sticks fell off. There were holes in his walls! Duncan howled.

Olive was a wise owl. She knew to make a house out of bricks. However, Olive was not strong enough to carry bricks. Harry and Duncan were, though.

"We can build a house together," Olive said. "Will you help me?"

Harry and Duncan helped Olive make a house out of bricks. No matter how hard the wind blew, their house stayed strong!

33

1. Three friends wanted to build houses because

   a. they liked the farm.

   b. they wanted to make new friends.

   c. they wanted to stay safe.

2. Why did Harry make a house out of straw?

   a. Straw was strong.

   b. He liked to eat straw.

   c. He did not know what else to use.

3. Why did Duncan build a house of sticks?

   a. Because the sticks were strong.

   b. Because he did not like straw.

   c. Because he loved to fetch sticks.

4. Why did Olive need help from her friends?

   a. Because she could not carry bricks on her own.

   b. Because she was afraid.

   c. Because she did not know what to do.

5. Why couldn't the wind knock over Olive's house?

   a. Because the wind did not blow hard enough.

   b. Because brick is strong.

   c. Because the friends worked together.

Name_____

Read the story. Write the answers to the cause and effect questions.

• •

Camillo had an idea. His school did not have a soccer team. He and his friends could make their own league. The neighborhood had enough kids for four teams. His friends agreed. "What a great idea!" they said.

It took all day to clear a vacant lot. Camillo wanted the field to be smooth.

"Nobody will want to play on a bad field," Camillo said. "We have to make it fair." He made sure the goal posts were the same on each side. He counted his steps to measure the field. He made sure the ball had lots of air.

When the day came for the first game, everybody came. They all wanted to play, even Camillo. But he did not.

"Why won't you play?" a friend asked.

"Because we need rules," Camillo said. "So today, I'll be the ref."

His friend, Ben, smiled. "I'll do it next time," he said.

Camillo smiled back.

1. Why did Camillo and his friends make their own league?

    _____

    _____

2. What did Camillo think would be the effect of a bad field?

    _____

    _____

3. What caused Camillo to choose not to play?

    _____

    _____

4. When Camillo's friend said he would be ref next time, what was the effect?

    _____

    _____

Perry's Treasure Hunt

Read the story. Circle the clue words (**because**, **why**, **when**, and **so**) in the story. Answer the cause and effect questions on the next page.

• •

One spring day, Perry Packrat said, "I think I will go looking for things. I need more stuff to put in my room."

Perry walked down the forest trail. She took her wagon so she could put all the things she found in it.

Perry looked to the left. She looked to the right. She looked up above her. She looked down at her feet. She saw a stack of bottle caps. She scooped them up and put them in her wagon.

"No, no! Don't take my bottle caps!" yelled Sammy Squirrel. "I am going to paste them on a picture for my teacher. That is why I have been saving them."

Perry walked down the path with her wagon. She saw a stack of newspapers in front of Rick Raccoon's den. So, she asked, "Do you need all these papers, Mr. Raccoon?"

"I am saving them so I can start warm fires this winter. I need them," he said.

Perry was sad because she wanted the papers, too. She walked on. When she saw some pretty flowers, she wanted to pick them for her mother. Her mother loved flowers.

Perry started to pick a flower. A bee buzzed by. "Please do not pick the flowers. I need the flowers so I can make honey."

Perry went home with her empty wagon.

Mama opened the front door. "Where have you been?" she asked.

She saw Perry's empty wagon. Mama smiled because she was happy. Perry had not come home with more trash!

Perry's Treasure Hunt (cont.)

Answer the questions about the story on the previous page.

• •

1. Why did Perry take her wagon? _____

   _____

2. Why had Sammy saved the bottle caps? _____

   _____

3. Why did Rick Raccoon need the papers? _____

   _____

4. Why did the bee need the flowers? _____

   _____

5. What made Mama smile? _____

   _____

Write On!

Read the sentence pairs below. Combine the two sentences into one sentence that tells cause and effect. Use a cause and effect clue word. **Because, so, why,** and **when** are clue words.

1. Tony spilled his milk.

   Mom got mad.

   _____

   _____

2. The big black dog barked at Tina.

   She ran home crying.

   _____

   _____

3. The little bird could not get back to its nest.

   It could not fly.

   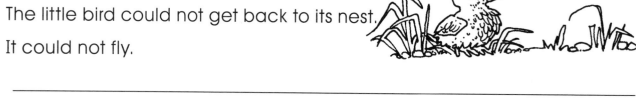

   _____

   _____

4. Joan kicked the ball into the street.

   She ran to tell the teacher.

   _____

   _____

Chain Reaction

Read the story. Answer the cause and effect questions.

• •

Terry dropped the marble. It hit the sleeping cat on the nose. The surprised cat jumped on the dog's tail. The dog yipped and chased the cat. The cat ran under the fish tank. The fish tank shook back and forth. Water and one small fish splashed out onto the floor. The thirsty dog lapped up the water.

1. Why did the dog lap up the water? _____

   _____

2. Why did the fish tank wobble? _____

   _____

3. Why did the dog chase the cat? _____

   _____

4. Why did the cat jump on the dog's tail? _____

   _____

5. What caused the chain reaction? _____

   _____

What Animals Can Do

Read the article. Remember that causes and effects can sometimes tell us why something cannot happen. Answer the cause and effect questions at the bottom of the page.

• •

Animals find ways to live in their worlds. Pandas live in jungles with lots of bamboo. They eat bamboo. Other animals, like cows, cannot eat bamboo. It is too tough for them to chew! Cows live on grassy plains, so they eat grass. Rabbits like vegetables.

Animals also have to drink. In the desert there is very little water. Camels can store water in their humps. One big drink can last a camel a very long time. Desert lizards can live on almost no water at all. But cows and pandas need lots of water. They cannot store it.

Animals have to keep warm, too. The arctic is very cold. Polar bears live in the arctic. They have thick fur to keep them warm. Seals and whales have blankets of fat. That keeps them warm too. Not all animals have fur and fat to keep them warm.

1. Why do camels store water? _____
   _____

2. Why would a panda have a hard time living in a desert? _____
   _____

3. Why can't cows eat bamboo? _____
   _____

4. Why can a seal live where it is cold when a lizard cannot? _____
   _____

Name _____

Read the stories. Circle the answers to the cause and effect questions.

• •

Pumpkin Pie

Jake wanted pumpkin pie. He planted his pumpkin and kept it in his bedroom. When it got bigger, he moved it to the greenhouse. In the summer, he moved it to the garden. He built a fence around it. The pumpkin got huge! One night in the fall, Jake woke up. He was shivering. There was a frost. This was not good for the pumpkin. In the morning, he went out to the garden. His pumpkin was black and squishy. There would be no pumpkin pie!

1. Why did Jake not have any pumpkin pie?

    a. Someone stole his pumpkin.

    b. There was a frost.

    c. He did not take care of it.

    d. The pumpkin got too big.

Ella's Luck

Ella threw her apple core in the bushes. The apple core had seeds that grew into a little tree. Years passed. She grew older. She got married. The house she grew up in was her house now. In the backyard was a big tree that filled with ripe fruit every fall. Her children brought it inside. They made apple pies!

2. Why did Ella get to make apple pie?

    a. She got married.

    b. Bushes grew bigger.

    c. Seeds from her apple core grew into a tree.

    d. Her children grew up.

Deserts on the Map

Read the article. Look at the map. Answer the cause and effect questions on the next page.

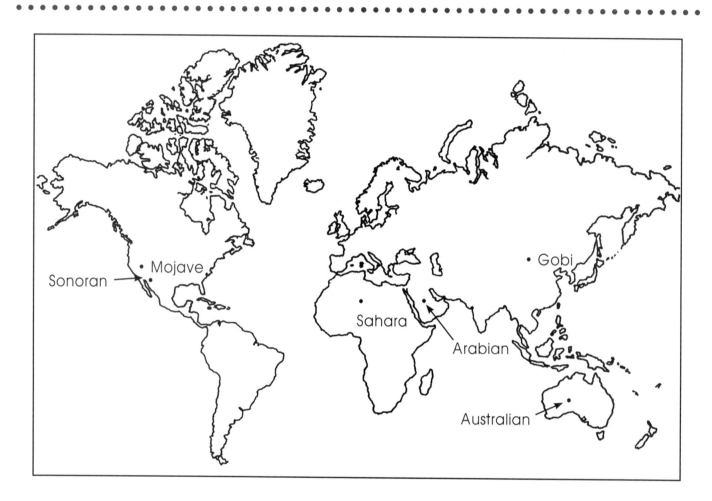

Deserts are dry places. They get less than 10 inches (25 cm) of rain every year.

The Mojave and Sonoran Deserts are in a rain shadow. A rain shadow happens near mountains. The desert is on the dry side of the mountain. The rain falls on the other side.

Some deserts are very big. The biggest ones are the Sahara, the Australian, and the Arabian deserts. They are near the equator. It is very hot and dry there.

The Gobi Desert in China is dry, too. It is not near the equator. It is dry because it does not get a lot of rain. It is too far from the ocean.

Not all deserts are hot. Some deserts are too cold for plants to grow.

Deserts on the Map (cont.)

Circle the correct answers to the questions below.

1. A place is called a desert when

   a. it gets less than 10 inches (25 cm) of rainfall per year.

   b. it is a hot place.

   c. it is close to the equator.

2. The Arabian Desert is hot and dry because

   a. it is in a cold place.

   b. it is near the equator.

   c. no plants can grow there.

3. The Mojave Desert does not get a lot of rain because

   a. it is in a cold place.

   b. it is near the equator.

   c. it is in a rain shadow.

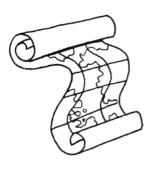

4. Why is the Gobi a desert?

   a. The desert has mountains all around it.

   b. It is near the equator.

   c. It does not get much moisture from the ocean.

43

Name _____

Read each part of the story. Complete the sentences that explain cause and effect.

• •

1. Trish put on her hat and coat. "I'm going to the library," she said to her mom.

    "Why?" her mom asked.

    "I'm doing a project for the school science fair. It's about stars. I need a book so I can plan my report."

    The librarian showed Trish where to look for books about stars. She found three books and checked them out.

    Trish checked three books out of the library because _____

    _____

    _____

2. When she got home, Trish sat down in her favorite chair and began to read. She read that the sun is the closest star to Earth.

    "Hey, Mom," Trish said. "Did you know that our sun is a star?"

    "It's a very important star," Mom said.

    Trish made a poster of the sun for her star project.

    Trish _____

    _____ because the sun is a very important star.

3.   Trish lived in the big city. One clear night, she went out in her backyard and looked up at the sky. She tried to count the stars. They were hard to count because of all the city lights.

   "Mom, where can I see lots and lots of stars?" she asked.

   "You can see stars when we go to Grandpa's house," Mom told her.

   "When can we go?" Trish asked.

Trish wanted to go to Grandpa's house because _____

_____

4.   The next Saturday, Mom and Trish drove to Grandpa's house. He lived out in the country on the top of a hill. There were no houses or stores near his house.

   "Grandpa," Trish said. "Mom said I would see lots of stars here."

   Grandpa looked up at the sky. "There are no clouds tonight, so we will see lots of stars. I have a special surprise for you, too."

   "What is it, Grandpa?" Trish asked.

   "Wait until it gets dark." Grandpa said.

   When they went outside after dark, Trish saw more stars than she could count. Then Grandpa showed Trish the surprise. It was a telescope that would help her see the stars even better.

Trish _____

because there were no clouds in the sky.

Answer Key

Page 4
1. c, e; 2. e, c; 3. c, e

Page 5
1. cause: Miguel poured food into a dish; effect: His dog jumped up and wagged its tail. 2. cause: Her cat climbed down from the tree; effect: Mary was happy. 3. cause: The hamster wanted some cheese; effect: The hamster climbed a ladder. 4. cause: Amy had an apple; effect: The pony ran to the fence.

Page 6
Circle: 1. happy; 2. sad; 3. sad; 4. sad; 5. happy

Page 7
1. good dog; 2. good dog; 3. good dog; 4. bad dog; 5. bad dog; 6. bad dog

Page 8
1. cause: rain; effect: wet; Rain makes you wet. 2. Cause: sun; effect: hot; The sun makes you hot. 3. cause: seed; effect: tree; You must plant a seed to grow a tree.

Page 9
1. could not find syrup; 2. can have pancakes; 3. does not eat meat; 4. made a tasty sandwich

Page 10
Circle: 1. mittens, boots, jacket; 2. sweater, pants, shoes; 3. shorts, sunglasses, sun hat; 4. raincoat, umbrella, rain boots

Page 11
1. c, e; 2. e, c; 3. c, e; 4. e, c; 5. c, e

Page 12
Draw Lines: 1. b; 2. a; 3. d; 4. c

Pages 13–14
1. e, c; 2. c, e; 3. e, c; 4. e, c

Page 15
Circle: 1. t-shirt and shorts; 2. raincoat and umbrella; 3. scarf, mittens, hat

Page 16
Circle: 1. effect, cause; 2. cause, effect 3. effect, cause

Page 17
Circle: 1. b; 2. a; 3. b

Page 18
Draw Lines: 1. e; 2. c; 3. a; 4. b; 5. d

Page 19
Draw Lines: 1. c; 2. a; 3. d; 4. b

Page 20
1. Huge Baby Weighed; 2. Kids Clean Up; 3. Grass Turns Yellow; 4. Boy Saves Dog; 5. Wind Blows House Down

Page 21
1. hot day; 2. to make sure it was safe; 3. a hippo at the watering hole

Page 22
Circle: 1. Waves form. 2. The waves get bigger. 3. People have to leave the beach.

Page 23
Circle: 1. so; 2. because; 3. when; 4. because; 5. because
Write: 1. cause: I did not mow the lawn; effect: I cannot play. 2. Cause: my tire hit a rock; effect: I fell off my bike. 3. cause: I laughed at my brother; effect: Mom was mad. 4. cause: the dog growled at me; effect: I ran away. 5. cause: you are funny and nice; effect: I am your friend.

Page 24
1. He was too hungry; 2. She did not make notes.

Page 25
1. d; 2. a; 3. b; 4. c

Page 26
Draw Lines: 1. c; 2. e; 3. d; 4. a; 5. b

Page 27
1. They forgot their tent; 2. Dad said they could sleep on the ground; 3. The sky was their tent; 4. Answers will vary.

Page 28
Circle: 1. a, d, e; 2. a, c

Page 29
Circle: 1. b; 2. b; 3. a; 4. b

Page 30
1. Lisa thought Jayla was nervous; 2. she wanted to help Jayla; 3. knew she would try to score; 4. she helped a friend.

Page 31
Circle: 1. a; 2. c; 3. a

Page 32
Circle: 1. b; 2. a; 3. b

Pages 33–34
Circle: 1. c; 2. b; 3. c; 4. a; 5. b

Page 35
1. Their school did not have a soccer team. 2. Nobody would want to play on it. 3. They needed rules so he would be the ref. 4. Camillo smiled.

Page 36
Circle: so, why, when, because

Page 37
1. She could put all the things that she found in it. 2. He was going to paste them on a picture for his teacher. 3. He was saving them to start warm fires in the winter. 4. She needed the flowers so she could make honey. 5. Polly had not come home with any more trash.

Page 38

Answers will vary. Possible answers are:
1. Mom got mad because Tony spilled his milk. 2. The big black dog barked at Tina, so she ran home crying. 3. The little bird could not get back to its nest because it could not fly. 4. Joan kicked the ball into the street, so she ran to tell the teacher.

Page 39

1. The dog was thirsty. 2. The cat ran under it. 3. The cat jumped on the dog's tail. 4. It was surprised. 5. Terry dropped the marble.

Page 40

Answers will vary. Possible answers:
1. Camels store water so they can live in the desert. 2. Deserts do not have bamboo or enough water.
3. Bamboo is too tough for cows to chew. 4. Seals have fat to keep them warm and lizards do not.

Page 41

Circle: 1. b; 2. c

Pages 42–43

Circle: 1. a; 2. b; 3. c; 4. c

Pages 44–45

Answers will vary. Examples:
1. she was doing a project on stars; 2. made a poster of the sun; 3. she could see the stars there; 4. could see lots of stars

Cause and Effect • CD-104550